NATURAL DISASTERS

For Rochelle & my mother

". . . the dizzying array of forces which
conspire together for our destruction. . ."
André Bréton

Contemporaries

NATURAL DISASTERS

Terry Stokes

New York University Press
New York 1971

Copyright © 1971 New York University
Library of Congress Catalogue Card
Number: 72-166522

ISBN: 0-8147-7754-6

Manufactured in the United States of America

Some of these poems have appeared in the following anthologies and magazines: New Generation Of Poets; Michigan Signatures; Poets, Kalamazoo; Ann Arbor Review; Choice; North American Review; Sumac, Red Clay Reader; Red Cedar Review; Hearse; Field; Arx; Westigan Review; Chelsea; Back Door; Baby John Got Shot On His Way To The West; The Miscellany; Esquire; Sou'Wester.

The following poems were included in the chapbook, *Living Around Other People,* Westigan Review Press: "Birds," "The River Dredger," "On Living Around Other People," "The Girl With Buckteeth & other dreams," "For The Guy Who Wrote The Dictionary."

TABLE OF CONTENTS

I

II

94325

III

IV

NATURAL DISASTERS

As I piece together people of the past,
they become strangers. Somehow, eyes
 & lines of faces shift, & I fall out
of love with the simplicity of flesh.

Singling out several who fell down
the steps getting up in the world,
twisting their fate so they look good on paper
as if they went to town with their lives,
bought goods for strayed souls.

Some surely followed the straight & narrow
 & bored themselves to death.
Others watched & waited
for the bone dust to collect in their rooms.

For the ones who wrestled with the lion
 & let the strong claws sink in,
smothered by love & muscles,
I etch you calmly, clearly
so the sun may settle full on your forms.

Everybody wants a little something
from the house of death.
They died, those old people, & they left
their lives behind. An electric toaster,
a thing that puts candles out. I get the old man's suit,
double-breasted, in season. I bring you to
the house of death, come, choose something for yourself.
How about the Family Bible? It's old,
worth something in the hock shop.
Slides of a sad cruise to warm islands.
I brought few ladies to the house of death,
furnished without love, impossible to build anything
that was not there.
The old man died in bed. The old woman fell
while watering plants, broke her heart in two.
The flower-room died that day. Everything genuine
cut-glass. I face you through the streams of memories
you cry all night & on through the day.
Out of the sick chamber,
out of the death palace
into a world filled with heavy snow.
You see only wet snowflakes on your nose, you become gray,
you have always been happy this way.
I could make a noise that would threaten your breasts,
bring you close at hand. I continue to love
scarred women, they never have to be healed.
My life, quiet old Testament.
Snow piles, the plow's been through town.
I was so young, I was not even thinking dirty hands,
or electric shaver or any of the things
I can now easily have. They would tell me how bad
not to finish the cereal, how bad to pick my nose,
how bad to be such a little boy in a house
filled only with antiques, you want to run away.
& you come back shivering, not with cold anymore,
with anxiety, trying to crowd out the stiff furniture.

Instead, you rearrange everything, you love nothing.
Pry open the helpless closets as if
they were the eyes of the long dead
about to give you new life.

NOBODY TO DO HER UP RIGHT

Frodo & other Lilliputians
lived around the house,
& left their wet marks
on the walls, ceilings,
all over the flowered bedsheets.
Dawn was part of garbled gestures
people who went away
or stayed too long
& slit wrists when everything else
had been cut-up
for food.
She studied mother-pig
at birth-time. Learned the names of trees, birds,
though words were not any kind of tool
for spreading open the cosmological eye.
Natural objects do
not think
but through our flesh vision
flash their colors. Listen.
The last tuning, a short rush,
an accident,
burned-out vibrations
& body sugar,
& stopped the blood rivers
before the quaking dam.

AUNT ELENORE

I knew her only as
stinking flesh & skin
stretched over small bones
& they wanted me to kiss her
she called me beautiful child
her mouldy hands pressed me
I thought of warts & sweet
vomit—she pissed in bed.
Orange flesh in the orange room
nearly the mystery of the temple
across the street,
the moaning men:
they gave me the scares
they were magicians
they did not make her well
she stayed the same
rotting
& I in all sorts of light since
have kissed bodies
bad & dead.

11

SO SIMPLE THE SADDER PEOPLE

I see her every time I eat a sandwich,
she is between bread, she was always
filling things out. She wore her skirts
lower; from a fertile family.
The old hardon would come rising up,
singing songs, she misunderstood,
as a matter of act, her fat sisters would
have understood better. They had the shape
of babies in their bellies before they were born, I'm sure.
They had a careless way of letting slide
several inches of thigh, every time there
was something to be done with their skirts.
They were sexy in their time; from a poor family.
A younger brother, there were many of them,
lifted in air by a fat cow, swirled several times,
his balls crushed, I couldn't look at him
after that, could you? & the mother grew
fatter, laughed at always at the center store, &
the father thin forever, laughed at always at the center
store & the house burned down & everyone
for a week was willing to take a child,
a fat child a thin child & care a little for it.
& the younger brothers never got older,
how much heaven for the poor & fertile family?
They have no name here or there.

WHAT SHE DID WITH THE SNAKE

She killed a copperhead when she was a counselor.
I think with her hands.
Perhaps with her teeth.

What she really did was throw a rock
a hundred feet
right into his left eye.
A lopsided snake always
keeps his brain there just in case.
& she took the kids for a hike,
& one with orange hat & teeth said,
"a sn-n-n-nake," & counselor, eyes creaming,
said, "it is a copperhead."
& picked up the brick I mentioned
before . . .

to cut the story short:
the kids were never frightened again.
They took pieces of the fat sick snake home
when camp closed.

They forgot her. But watch—
they rub always the soft snake skin on their breasts
as the moon shimmies in the sky
& winks with its one good eye.

TREES FROM SOME PAST LIFE

As the eyes mate with the sockets,
you decode the seasons.
Trees from some past life, saps, pines,
& the hills they rolled with
& climbed.

Like Christ spiked, crisp blood on snow
below the balcony on 82nd,
as I writhe in pain &
preparation for church.

Dogs eat the ale-wives, a foot high
on the shores, stuffed deep in the sand.

The father of the flesh has left
dragging mother, hair filled with dead flowers,
vines too strange to untangle.
The air is fresh, cold for spring.
Along the shoals, they fade in the fog,
leave sweet thorns in the wake.

Mania, my lion,
we walk the blood-filled streets of summer,
sucking the seedless fruits of the future,
nodding to the winemakers.

IT IS NOT HALLOWEEN

Your eyes rode the straight & narrow,
no need for brains,
you had a party dress, pink, I think,
& orange teeth,
it was not Halloween.
You screeched, Creep, Reap.
I jumped, my hand harvesting
hair, the juices I didn't know where they were
exactly, you led me by smell,
I said, what the hell,
my voice cracked.
Get Out Of The Hayloft, your grandma yelled.
Was I in deep? Messing up the hay?

I went away to study sin, sex, fragrances
of the fall, stiff leaves.
Today, soft when the tractors come with bales
& the old ladies croak,
I smoke a little corn silk & set your barn on fire.

THE GRANDMOTHER

The man, Brown, strange name for a Jew,
the grandmother said in her subtle bloodless
Christian voice, bought the house,
swimming pool & hedge next door.

Her DAR meetings, bridge games suffered,
his smiling Hasidic face wailing
through her windows.

She loved squirrels, pear trees,
& a good book,
but where to spend her sermons? Her psalms?

He added on to his house, a wife &
a couple of daughters in good faith,
planted his own strange seeds.

Old Granny rocked away her days, her hate,
waiting for heaven,
lost her sight in the stiff bushes
growing toward the light.

Her name was the same as mine.
I liked him. He was small. The scooter,
a most valuable player, he could move to the left,
to the right, just as well. Leaping through
the reality of my baseball cards, about as high &
fast as anybody.

I had a hang-up about Italian girls in those days.
I loved her. She was Catholic. & when we played
marriage, it was one hell of a time.
What with cloth over our heads, & she wouldn't
kiss me cause, it wasn't for real, though I followed
the ritual exactly, or as far as she explained it.
It was a lot of gigles for little kids.

Bouncing the rubber ball off the side of the house,
& fielding every impossible play, as the ball
scratched the sky, or shivered in the grass.
I saw myself as big-time. I went on to smoke
at an early age, & couldn't even run around
the field at fifteen. Maybe, the great junk pitcher,
knuckle-balls, screw-balls, & a change-up, when hit,
out of the park. I had control problems. So.
I practiced Pepper Martin, it was a gas, spikes high,
shearing the jersey-socks of the unsuspecting
second baseman. I didn't get on base that often.
& the coach chased me around the high school
parking lot just to watch the smoke pour from my ears.
I got hurt bunting once. He didn't give me much
sweat after that. I saw baseball as fun & games.

The last time I saw Phil Rizzuto's daughter was
in a magazine. It was the only time. She had black
curly hair & smiled a lot.

She was 12, an older woman,
skinny with buckteeth,
& a dirty black pony-tail, & she fell
every night
from a tree onto some rocks,
nearly,
but of course I caught her,
& gave her my I.D. bracelet.
It wasn't a bad dream at all.

Snake dreams followed.
Harmless, but clustered
the way snakes will
when they seek warmth, &
I would wake, never leaving
the bed, they were under it,
like the unused train set,
another snake-gift from my father,
not poison, just swirls in my nest.

& then, there were no dreams
to speak of,
the guillotine sliced my neck
like warm bread, & I never knew
who was holding the string,
a quiet trickle of blood, a thread,
rose easily on white flesh
in a soft room.

I do not remember the dreams which surrounded
the suicide attempt,
the search for fire escapes, naked,
the doctor thought that would keep me down,
bruised but nothing broken as usual.
I flap about for the girl with the buckteeth,
like bird eggs dropping on the rocks
soon, her red crinolines will splash
right outside my fragile home.

BLOODSUCKERS

Skinny-dipping is some sport
in the ball-busting cold streams
of the Berkshires, the foothills.
You go with your friend, an old man,
or so he seems, he's even seen
the fuzz between girls legs &
how they fall apart if you touch them deeply.
The day is hot as hell.
So, you cool off.
The clothes first.
& you wonder if you're the only circumcised kid
in the country & more serious problems
of status, but it's only cause you're little.
So. The plunge.
& you shrivel up as the goose pimples grow,
& he says something about bloodsuckers
& since you're prone to blood
rushing to your head,
scared of anybody leeching
any of your strength,
you wade out for a moment,
& face the five extra protrusions,
pulsing, testing, your still
undeveloped life.

MOTHER

The flowers in my mother's dress
were so soft
as my head drowned in her lap
they were like fields in a slow motion movie,
a slight haze over everything.
& we watched morning stars
guide us through ragweed, Indian paintbrush,
in soft Connecticut spring.
& my sister, exactly my age,
was with us all the way,
frightened eyes as the caterpillars
scratched her short legs,
startled by the quickness, the coolness of life
as she would slip out of the tube,
learning to swim,
in the cold brooks cut between glacial rocks,
& she would cry for air
from the bottom.
Mother sure in the water, would dive down
& drag her to shore
where the sobs would shake the trees,
& the fish would spring for flies,
& the sun setting
shook shadows
from the fast moving stream.

These days, my mother having shaken
the shadow of a second husband
resides in another quaint Connecticut town
where art like life flourishes in the summer.
Her second batch of children are more sensible,
they don't fall into much trouble.
All the tubes are gone,
though her eyes follow their forms clearly.

She is still strong,
poised to dive,
poised to pick flowers
should the season ever change,
should the waters ever rise
over their heads.

Mississippi River—Iowa-Illinois border
I'm on a trip & my bags are a day behind.
The lady, 'You must be new in town,'
"No," bag in hand, me.
I wish I were going to see the Marx brothers
with her—am glad I'm on the bus.
The driver & I talk over
sinuses over egg salad sandwiches,
how can he risk those farts
on these long drives?
Little lady obviously psychotic
changes seats each time
Dianne & I laughed—Dianne
married a diplomat who put
a baby between her neck & knees
as she was six feet—she could never
possibly understand me.
My grandparents did a lot of busing
but she hated it—hurt her leg
one time—told my grandfather to go alone
hoping for promiscuities—he didn't
she hated hot weather—he loved Florida,
55 years of quibbling & snoring together
& me the last of their children
who reveled in warm climates & things.
They would be sure I was going
the way of my father
which they would say
bad terrible drunkard &
no job, how much can he
love his children? Did he
love them by staying away
& you would not let him see me
he would become over-emotional,
I am seven wearing my sister's skirt
something is missing.

The clouds are crazy &
this mid-west bus makes me seasick
this mid-west makes me seasick
& now the billboards will say it's spring.
I would have grown into adult hog calling
but we went places nearly
as fast as possible.
47 years old & your collar crumpled
your breath stinks whiskey
& you like continually
shaking my hand—you do
it for hours—that is
each time I have swatted
your deliberately helpless
fingers off my thigh—the
back seat close to the john &
uncomfortable.
The mid-west's lights
are going off—still
more in my thoughts than love
are the rainstorms—the monsoon
seasons of the soul—these are the gentle times
of soft slow ever present passion
& nothing makes sense.
It is gusty—fever climbs
the body evenly & the eyes drown
sloppily we understand rides
we take for father, freedom, love
are just dreams
are only earth moving
beneath us.
I just hope no beautiful woman
falls into my hot lap
I would tell her everything
the sirens wailing & we
the near escapees.
Now, Chicago & night
a sandwich, a beer

this is it the wait
is right & long.
She orange hair
eyes tinted orange
dress spitting orange
breasts—the pass spent
in urine much to the delight
of the nervous washroom.
Three egg conversations:
one bacon & eggs
one fried eggs
one poached.
An anecdote:
she slept at my side
warm the bus ride
& left so early in the morning.
Chattanooga, plateau life
they hate here as much as eyes allow.
A few laughs
he going to see mother die
of cancer never smoked
that's the way it goes
slowly
giving me cigarettes
his chestnut face caught
in a bad white land.
The bus, all of us
like hawks, eyes & talons
strained, squealing
tires & chickens,
a little killing
on a hairpin turn.
Sit down
pink & white tall
easter outfit
out of the haze of Tennessee's mountains
this is the only empty seat.
Chew gum & I will go into

sleep against the window away
from you & your book, *Alcoholic Wife,*
Which you think, a pretty good book
I might like to read.
No thanks, I'm toying
with the hem of your black hair
which gets fast dirty
at the end of the assembly line
weekdays in Toledo, Ohio,
my eyes still closed
my mouth grinding
a piece of your gum.
This is night
it is bitter almonds
I do not know where I am going
I do not know.
This is easy with my bags
a full day behind.
Beware
beware the easy sky
graying at the temples
Annie's long blonde hair
wet from the hot day
her thighs sticky with my
strawberry ice cream & cone
I pulled the buzzer & slipped
away with her thoughts trickling
down my back at the next bus stop.
So here I am splitting dark
in sunny Florida on an air-conditioned bus,
'Visit the scrub pines
The House of Dishes
Visit the sand ·
The Y.M.C.A.' & so little time
with my bags a day behind.
Sweet corn
in the morning
sweet corn in the morning

& the sky blacking out
with the songs of the fruit farms
& the fields of the cattle & birds.
Suppose we were to put on
our racing feet & tear away
the woods with our loins,
what then love, more woods?
It is still
this air
still with soot & juices still
not flowing. The awnings & the trees
hung with slim leaves
we are all of the same age & feminine
in this silent air. The single gray
a highway: where it all happens
with my bags a day behind
but on the way.
This highway
with stops
in & out of day & night
in & out of weather
I am your baggage
& you take me along
in & out of yourself
between orange peels
above the water
dark with itself.

II

THE DERVISH WHIRLS

As the wind of winter gets stronger
& whaps right through
the windows, I fumble with cold shadows.
Crossing the room, the light, on,
I deal the voice his card,
fry him in butter & call him love.

It is so wrong.

The dervish whirls, & whispers as I knot
his neck,
break it. He waddles alone into
the paths of fast moving cars.
How would he know the darkness, its broken nevers,
its striated longings, or the bumper
which ends it all.

All judgement lost in trials.

He would wage war.
"You are loose." "Not Guilty."
"Unity?" "The arrow flies
its own way toward the undiscovered heart."
Listen.
The arms of the child have loved things, too,
for instance, the color blue.
He fell for the sky. It was that simple.
out there. His hair stood straight,
but that was good, his head like frigid
marbles, & the kite, his strange connection,
flew from his hands, landed in the untrimmed tree.
He prayed long & loud in the sun.

He fought the music.

We will not live with the magic, love,
& we will not stay at the fair.
I untie the sash of your robe,
throw the rings in the air.
As mythical night
lurches like some mad ship,
we dance our strange route through the desert.

THE CONSISTENCY OF THE HEART

Who could swallow it all? The whole story:
a man is trapped in a vat of anchovies,

is becoming, unless, of course, the firemen can save him, a tin of Fish
Delight. His name is Jesus,
of Mexican descent. Ah, the tales he will spin

for his children who could possibly be eating
his legs out of brown bags in school lunchrooms,

saying, the sweet taste of the ocean
slips through our teeth, & the texture

is that of the salmon's heart, broken
on his way upstream, visits to loved ones
are always this way,

& the wails for a new life, pink
as the flesh we search for.

REALITY CABBAGE

for John Berryman

Your mistress they liked,
held her close so she wouldn't get out of hand,
something to do with their lines.

But you & your ruler & the bones
was too rich, bubbles, & dreams,
for the blood.

I bury the head in sleep,
reality cabbage
cruel enough for love.

"I DON'T KNOW WHY YOU SAY GOOD-BYE, I SAY HELLO."—The Beatles

After rinsing
the gray matter
oh, fourteen times or so,
"she's still a mystery
to me." & I'm all wet,
& not clean.

Look into the grass,
do you see the stars?
Or is the wall
filled with still bland flowers?
My wrists still hold
the scars
of love, yes,
love lost
to a stocky marine
who knew more than
feel-up in the movies.

& I thought,
if I wear the T-shirt backward,
it will be higher on the neck,
& that will do it.

Ha ha she laughed,
ha ha she skipped:
you can rub my legs,
& you can milk my thighs,
but that fella
in that uniform,
he fucks
out
my eyes.

Buttered popcorn
dribbled
from our teeth.
Fast tongues
slid
across the screen.
& I saw how screwed-up
it was,
& pushed the blade
to the flesh,
shooting pool,
one calm day.
It is a thousand dirty years later,
& there should be no war or
guilt implied.

THE NEIGHBOR LADY

Works 16 hours a day washing dishes,
& tries to find time
to drink. & the Bali Hai bottles
clutter up the garbage can. She has the wart red
nose of her life.

Breaking the ashtrays, on the way to the car
on the way to her sister's, the only living
relative, making them took days
in the fog, "Boy, that's really the shit."

My wife has winced & caught her
in the snow, bathrobe open,
singing to the moon.

Wrinkled hands stuffed in baggy pockets,
an overcoat night. Around the block & back
to the shower & bed. Lines almost made
the eyes disappear, a nose that rattled
as he blew it: reasons not to die,
I suppose.

      Wishes lost with the last child,
a tricky car accident, something to do with snow
& speed & a son bent for Omaha of all places.

Counting out the cracks in the sidewalk, he missed
the squirrel, curously circling the old tree on
the corner, waiting for nuts to grow or fall down.
A small flurry also whirled.

      Slipping, he came around
the bend & back, no time for breaking in new shoes.
He brushed off the steps. Inside, a storm was soon
to start.

THE FARMER

1.
As he learned the land,
the animals came easy, goats, puppy dogs,
antelope.

2.
Animals regarded him
as a misplaced person,
his shaggy hair, his blue eyes.

3.
The wife rubbed herself with bear grease & waited.

THE GAMES PEOPLE PLAY

The taste of butter was on your lips.
I ate the toast off the plate,
& went out for a long hard run
in the winter. It was too cold
for anything else. As the stars
broke in the snow, I tasted salt.

The sweat off my brim was salt.
I brought the spit from my lips,
to my fingers, & rolled the cold
until with flakes, a ball of stars,
I hurled the whole thing toward the plate.
You, limber, the great swinger, hit a home run.

All the games we played, cold,
& competitive. I have a way with stars,
you said. As if that changed anything in the long run.
Like sprinkling salt
on the robin's tail in the spring. Lips,
have a way of passing the plate.

You wore your plate,
& filled my wounds with salt.
Sure, it stopped the blood from running
down my shirt, leaving stars
on shoes, cold,
as you smack your stiff lips.

Near the lips
of the cup. It's golf-time, gold-plated
your putter. You ran
the ball close as salt
on an egg. The iron was cold
& your words were quiet as stars.

A shotgun full of salt.
you fired. As I ran
toward the goal in the cold.
Game's over, from the lips
of the soggy spectators plated
with booze, an afternoon of super stars.

Where were you running with your bag of salt?
Dribbling from your lips, the sad stars.
Served on a plate, the puck is cold.

THE VOYEUR

He dreamed they built a building.
I guess it was an apartment.
& it was glass & fifty stories.
& it looked down on his house.

& from his bathroom, he would watch,
as the eggs were scrambled, & juice
swirled in the blender, & she didn't care
what she wore, it was breakfast,
& shells tinkled into the pan.

& from the kitchen, he watched the playrooms.
Nasty children picking noses when parents
weren't watching, spilling blocks, &
finger-painting each other's hair,
as silly putty bounced around the room.

& from his bedroom, he watches beds,
crashing, happiness abandoned,
skeletons rattling,
breaking the bones of love.

He dreams his eyes will not wake.

THE DEFINITIVE BIRD POEM

Lately it's been birds.
A red bird in the bush.
What kind? What kind?
He was a kind bird, staying long enough
to fill my eyes with his blood color
& wings which too bled,
as he nearly flew over houses.

The blue bird is not unlike other birds,
only he is blue,
& looks good against snow,
which is a problem for him
as he needs food, & other birds,
all colors, seem to stay away
which is to say
he is nasty, noisy, & quite alone.

The "it's" referred to in the opening line
must be explained:
Birds I see, too, as love,
or simply a streaking sign,
as we try to pinpoint what love must look like
or feel like.
It's like the food the pelican keeps
in his unhinged jaw,
it's sitting there,
waiting to foul up,
waiting to be eaten if not digested.

Much too long a poem,
birds don't deserve it.

"IT ISN'T THE CLOTHES YOU WORE,
THAT SOON WENT OUT OF STYLE"—The Montanas

Going up the road,
angel in mouton.
Wing it, baby,
sing your song.
Break open your wrapped parcels
of fear, dear.
Old notions, motions,
& sprigs of trees
out the window
lying plain on the lawn,
lying on the ground,
lying on the earth,
lying.
Bird shit & dog sperm
boil in the sun,
but to love that, too,
you have to dig dirt.
First, you fell
for Kansas City, then it was Dubuque,
after that Albuquerque,
somebody who ran a Burger-Chef
gave you a location,
no vacation, you called it
vocation, something to do
with yourself,
"rainy days come so often out here
I fear I've lost my heart."
In the morning,
working things out was easy,
one box of cereal on the shelf.
Afternoons,
one movie house.
Nights, & where to go,
what to do, neon
keeps flashing
all the news that's fit
to print.

III

THE FESTIVAL OF LIFE

As the festival of life
trickles down the warm Chicago drain,
& the nightsticks, click click,
on pavements once again,
he is quiet in his cell.

If you can't make the black creeps fall,
keep them off the streets, a kick in the groin,
some gas. Suspected B & E, the catch-all.
& finally, the charge: attempted jail-break. 1-5.
Be thankful you're alive.

Later, the deal came, without judges or juries
or any of the white graces. The prosecutor permits
him to take a rap of ten years
for crimes unsolved in the sovereign state.
Fears settled, in Indiana, of all places.

When he returns to the block,
his friends will be locked up or lying in blood,
& he will have, simply, lost his life.

FLOWERS SINK THEIR ROOTS

It was the crazy ladies of the DAR
who kept up
the Indian cemetery, scattered stones,
near the church in the wildwood
where John & Judith on June 8th, 1968,
married.
It was the church, filled with flute, sermon & sweat,
which seemed strange
not the sign which said, Mary Whitney
has cemetery clean-up duty, Monday.

The mad Christians always deal in death,
they have no feel for flesh.
Flowers sink their roots
& split as they strike
arrow-head,
bleached bones of the Narragansett.
Devoid of grass,
the paths which lead us
tie us to the story line we manufacture
away from the sun
which some other tribes still worship.
The circle completed
the ceremony begins,
far from the stones, bones,
or dead eyes, glaring.

GOD KNOWS, WE DO WHAT WE CAN

Whittling away with a knife,
he crafted a cross out of some soft wood.
Needled himself for the roughness,
& sent if off to a woman
who sat watching the windows
for her soldier son's return.
& she stuffed it in his stiff hands,
as he, too, came boxed &
wrapped in a soft warm flag.

"DON'T ENDANGER YOUR MOST VALUABLE POSSESSION, YOUR CREDIT RATING, PAY YOUR BILLS BY THE TENTH"—
Credit Bureau Public Service Announcement

When I wed the little lady,
her old man said, "She's got good teeth,
& a flair for fantasy." I built with all my hands
the marble house, to keep our cool records, shingles,
& mortgages warm.
        I got the dream-car, a steal,
for the stereo-tape-deck, & we could dance real good
on the magic backroads where we petted & I got my
first love-bite.
        Life does not change like the T.V.'s,
her teeth are still crass white, & she gnaws,
gnaws on her fantasies as I sleep.

THE FIREMAN

"He was, also, a part-time professional clown."

They dragged the lady body
from the house down the street. It was night.
Blood clot somewhere,
& stiff, too, the unborn child
scrambled, as the fireman, clown, abortionist,
fiddled with his costume.
A stunted laugh, a flame,
cracks in eternity.

They die addressing Rotary Club luncheons.
If someone were straight into their eyes
to say, You're, ah, gonna, ah, fall
into a plate of jello salad & cottage cheese
will cream from your ears
& that's the way the wife will remember,
Clarence Austin Matterson, Mayor
of Yummie, Michigan.
His eyelashes were stiff
with beef gravy, & all over his bald head,
The Sparrows, women's auxiliary,
were caressing, sweat & callouses
mixed with the graham cracker crust
of Martha's, quick & easy, pie,
The Sodomy Delight, the last thing
to ooze through his lips.

Fondness is an inescapable anteater
wandering our deserts. He snickers,
snick, snick, "& what do you know
of food, fat ones? I have licked
the shell of the ant, the slivers
of eyes, & wiped out whole colonies
with my sticky tongue. Once,
just the workers, whew,
share the wealth—queen
bitching & flapping about,
I killed her with my snout."

Did you know her?
Did you love her brother?
Days, hot ones, thighs
straddling my bike,
I raped her eight maybe ten times in the brush,
brush was nature for Sukie Jean, teen-age queen
for those who dream ripple-fuck.

Swimming. Pools of chlorine
indoors. Glassed & cozy.
Vapors & tan bodies
whisper my last wish,
having none of their own.

THE DEAD SHEEP OF SKULL VALLEY

"The Army has denied any connection with the deaths,
but Thursday said tests of lethal nerve gas had been
conducted at Dugway, March 13, the day before the sheep
began dying."—AP

Out in Mormon land,
6,400 sheep are stiff &
the air is no different tasting
than in downtown Salt Lake City.
More bad meat for the markets.
Sheep—any of a wide variety of cud-chewing
mammals related to the goats, with heavy wool,
edible flesh called mutton, and skin used in making
leather, parchment, etc.

& so it came to pass
the U.S. Army created a super sheep-killer, too.
"Never have to worry about those fucking sheep
anymore, cause problems, make nasty noises, dirty,
herd behaviour"—hung up officer,
dealing with the fact
that everytime the teacher read
Mary Had A Little Lamb,
bestial fantasies
flashed.

& it came to pass
every house
was given free of charge
four lamb chops, one very large sweater,
ten ashtrays of stretched skin
& crushed skull parts
& enough innocent blood
to last the lifetime of our totem
which is also a sickness.

In time, the sacrifice completed
a few of the boys came home
from the crusade
& pleaded ignorant
in the face of the plastic sacraments
& whips in hand
slaughtered all children under five
who wrote the words,
"Little sheeps are in my head,
Little sheeps are never dead."

THE STIFF BARRICADES

We are so locked
in our hermetically sealed little bodies,
the blood, the blood
must spit out, & white snow
seems right.

I have watched the children of the night
as they battle for their voices,
as they sing the songs of the flesh
they have never known. Nothing but
tattered clothes left, & they won't keep
nobody warm.

Some have hurdled the stiff barricades
& found father clutched, nasty in love,
& what to do with it. "Keep their hands tied,
zippers up, & hide the keys."

Enough. We loll in the soft arms of our women,
let them teach us the direction for our guns,
the pulse of our bones.

A POEM FOR SEALS ALL OVER THE WORLD

Oil from Santa Barbara is killing
seals on an off-shore island.

He's a sea mammal, dog-like head,
torpedo-shaped body & four webbed feet or flippers,
just in case you don't get a chance
to see one.

His eyes are greased shut,
but eyes open & death are two different things.
You can get a seeing-eye dog, a little white
fold-up cane, & learn to slip
through crowded streets.
Your sense of hearing improves,
pictures melt into the ears.

But this is irrelevant, right?
Seals like fish & water, petty concerns,
when you figure
the oil man is interested in car-gas,
pouring oil on troubled waters,
& by-products which
burn babies eyes out.

How big is the seal casket?
How much is a slick pelt worth?

IV

THE CARNIVAL OF COMBS

He is trying to be quiet,
but show up,
through style.
Does style shine?
Does style glow?
Who will love him when he gets old
or eats oranges by the pound?
It is good to live in a time
when everything can go up in smoke,
houses, trains, artifacts,
& still,
one can live on,
in spite of Kiddie Carnival Time,
when the supermarket parking-lot
is a rest home, too,
for rusty ferris wheels, &
three rings for a quarter
will get you
home, combs in hand,
counting change, your prizes,
& run through your hair
& the burning mirror
& peace is not apparent
when you win something you need.

Where have we come from?
When everything is read as image;
the heart, a sexual flower
is fed pernod, kool-aid,
& cotton candy is gross pink hair
devoured by innocent lips.

& what you win, a comb perhaps,
is only a token of what you could have won
if you practised more often,
doing it in the dark
so you get expert at it,
& can zap the Zen arrow into the Zen heart
of the Zen target
without blinking a bloody eye
because feeling is below
the bridge of the nose,
& also, goes to Kiddie Carnivals,
at least once a week
hoping to be stranded on the Tilt-A-Whirl
with 15 rotten oranges,
& combs enough to keep the simplest style in place.
When we run out of hoops,
we must find other ways
back into the parking-lot,
into the supermarket,
where the fruit seems to be vegetables,
& good ones, delicious, healthy,
may not be enough for change
though the lights radiate for 24 hours at a stretch,
& I am yawning, combing like crazy,
& feel like an 86 year old orange
with not a single skin left to lose, to shed.

GETTING MARRIED IN THE CEMETERY

According to the sexton, funerals
take precedence over weddings.

For months, I played pinball machines
& drank short beers
hoping to die or lose track
of the cheap artifacts.

Instead of death, the marriage came
with the black angel hovering over
the minister & my bride, white
on the startling summer day,
full of flowers & friends & relatives
gradually falling out of love.

Oh, we drank & posed & packed everyone away,
& headed back to the apartment
where we uncovered your dresses & slips
& bits of history
locking in order
& slept the still new life.

DRUGS FOR THE HEAD

In Needle Park, they are in love
so why not you & I, love?

I've been where they make pik-up stix.
& the colors, your eyes hurt
as you learn them.
As a weapon they are fragile,
but your heart is soft
if that is a virtue,
so are mudflaps, volleyballs, & sweatshirts,
but you're not in the same league.

The pedestrians walk in & out of my poems like friends,
assaulting me,
"here's your assault for the day, friend."
& here is your blue pik-up stick.
Will they ride a cock,
horse, to Banbury Cross?
Or just run around re-arranging furniture,
"the bed goes in the john,
the refrigerator in the study
for when the poet writes
it's better if he's full,
& if it's food, maybe he won't eat other things."

If I watch long enough you will break into a smile,
& put down the gun,
& then where would the game end?

I'm a great lover,
"not bad
when you've got your heart in it,"
as she knits, click, click,
a red bag
big enough for my head.

THE FLIGHT

Some things we will never survive
if we think about them:

Take planerides, going away
with ease, speed, comfort,
is how we explain it
to the travel agent.
& the blood swelters,
& the skin melts.
First-class magazines, oxygen guides,
& letters weigh you down.
I am deadly serious here,
it is my life as well as yours.

Do all the homes in the world
go 500 mph & so close to the sun?
& do I love this woman who winks,
& serves grape jam & toast?
& where is the parachute when
I don't want to live here anymore?

Can a breath of air kill you?
Like a deep-sea diver,
the bends,
swooning, dreaming, swimming,
in a green marble cloud.
The flight,
will it last forever?

WINTER, FLOWERS

Oh I would jot some kind of love poem,
it would be a snowfort frozen,
roses, & roses, red, growing
in the center,
petals falling, etc.
It would burn with words,
dancing, self-ironic.
I reached for your hand
& slid past,
too eager for the puck.
This is for my wife, you just don't
jangle words around for your wife.

The coffee full of booze
rests
on the desk
as the high intensity lamp
watches
whatever the typewriter is doing.

My lungs & kidneys are trying
to die,
& you love them.
Early in the morning you are awake,
thinking kidneys, thinking lungs.

We graze inside the snowfort awhile,
roses so right
when you need a symbol,
when you're hungry. Like slow flames
the flowers ooze
from our lips, curl in the wind.
White flags flash on white flesh.
Captured. We rebuild,
the solid ice keeps us warm.

BIRDS

My life is full of birds.
They point out the trees,
high tension wires where they rest.
I have learned the cats of the neighborhood this week.
Soon, we will fly.
Soon, we will hover over other
small animals.

THE RIVER DREDGER

Dredging the river
with my river dredger,
I am a hard worker.

Sifting silt so
there is actually a shore,
also, I wear a hard hat.

ON LIVING AROUND OTHER PEOPLE

One abortion after another
one
two three
four.

FOR THE GUY WHO WROTE THE DICTIONARY

I read your book
last week.
Not bad.

SKIN FLOWERS

Dragging phosphorescent rats through
the house. By the tails.

There are no nails to hold
some things together.

Snow water drools off
the roof next door. Red,

this is, sun setting through it.
A girl with silver hair

wanders under the blood,
a black coat, warm & comfortable,

shortly before Easter   .
is not a good sign, any way

you read it. Pebbles are not happy
ranked with flowers,

particularly rat flowers,
or the mossy groin which

springs up from the oddest soil
to burn, to scream rat screams.

Drenched, the baggy skin.
Thuds.

ROLLING ALONG

I walk the rolling, snow streets,
dreaming incantations,
"marble est petite,
the brakes are low,
cream cheese, crackers, & sunshine,
the dog is black, the Mackinaw Bridge
is lying in ten feet of water,
the brains of politicians are Fargo, North Dakota."

Women love me. I save them from the sane world.
Drooling, hunched in my own way,
arms dragging,
well-placed blackheads in the dawn,
as I yawn, & take it all in.
There goes the Whackie Bird, kids,
he's a link in the commercial network,
sun-up to sun-down, he follows signals.

When I drive my sleigh through town
they throw fruit-juice cans, splinters, crabs,
charge cards, even. My team, blinders in place,
knows the route, eats stray movie houses,
abuses sad fat ears, shakes horny tails

in the mayor's face. Such a disgrace.

I have lived the loss of my hair,
Scuttled ships too heavy with data.

Drugs now bead in my veins,
as the rain
melts some colorful part of the brain.

LIGHT SOURCES & VULTURES

As chair arms twisted into snakes,
& fireplace, wood, & flames.
A raw night caught between
booze & pills.
  Forcing the bookshelf
to shift, up down,
  I understand
the shadows of Prometheus Unbound.
Light sources sneak into my eyes.
Smiles are killers
  & justice allows killers
to love us first. For the part of my brain
burned up,
I dance, cold flesh
dangling
from glowing bones.

ASHES

Bound to the taste of ash.
He has never smelled anything but
things burning or having burned.
His breath is a forest smoldering.

He has come to think through
his mouth & his nose. The sky
is tasteless. A house full
of jello is bland. His hair
is dead, soot falls from each nostril
& forms piles.

His lungs are gravel pits. The stones
too hot to handle. There is nothing
to cultivate but a certain
continuous gray. & it will
spread itself.

Beware, veins that go cool in the night.
Beware, the smooth touch of ash.

THE WEEK THE NATURE CENTER WAS CLOSED

We slipped around the wooden fence,
& found several raccoons still
very much alive. Washing apples, eating apples.
& they touched us. It was a good day.

We looked around for signs
of other life. A chicken, hmmm.

A hawk caught in his wire tent,
dreaming fat rodents.

It was such a quiet day I forgot
all this until now.
It is dark. The night birds moan.